Jenny Vaughan

Wild Weather
HEAT WAVE

QEB Publishing

Copyright © QEB Publishing, Inc. 2008

Published in the United States by
QEB Publishing, Inc.
23062 La Cadena Drive
Laguna Hills, CA 92653

www.qeb-publishing.com

Library of Congress Control Number: 2008012596

ISBN 978 1 59566 587 4

Printed and bound in the United States

Author Jenny Vaughan
Consultant Terry Jennings
Editor Amanda Askew
Designer Mo Choy
Picture Researcher Claudia Tate
Illustrator Julian Baker

Publisher Steve Evans
Creative Director Zeta Davies

Picture credits (a=above, b=below)
Alamy David Wall 20a, WoodyStock 27b

Corbis Bruno Barbier/Robert Harding World Imagery 11a, Jose Fuste Raga 12, Kim Kulish
14, Paul A Souders 15a, CDC/Phil 17b, Bettmann 19a, Liba Taylor 20b, Frank Lukasseck
24, John Carnemolla 29a

Getty Images Daniel J Cox 1, 5b, 19b, 22b, AFP 25a

NASA/Goddard Space Flight Center 13b

Rex Features Sipa Press 4, Lewis Whyld 13a

Science Photo Library Lea Paterson 16

Shutterstock Celso Pupo 5a, Dhoxax 7a, Slowfish 7b, Kondrachov Vladimir 8b, Matt
Trommer 10a, Jaroslaw Grudzinski 10b, Simone van den Berg 11b, Sherri R Camp 15b,
Elena Elisseeva 17a, Gina Smith 18, Ilker Canikligil 21, Hagit Berkovich 22a, Thomas
Pozzo Di Borgo 23, Georgios Alexandris 25b, Pakhnyushcha 27a, Anthony Ricci 29b

Topfoto Mark Conlin V&W 26

Words in **bold** can be found in the glossary on page 30.

Contents

What is a heat wave?

A heat wave is a long period of unusually hot weather. Like other forms of extreme weather, it can affect the environment and human health.

RISING TEMPERATURES

A heat wave happens when a mass of unusually warm air stays still over the same place for days or even weeks, with no cooler weather. In parts of the world where the weather is frequently very warm, hot weather is not considered to be a heat wave. Elsewhere, the same temperatures, or even lower ones, are a heat wave, just because they are not normal.

▼ In Brazil, temperatures are about 86 degrees Fahrenheit on average in summer. Although this is very warm, it is normal for this area and people have adapted to the climate.

◄ Hot weather and low rainfall have led to low water levels in the San Gabriel Reservoir, California.

THE HEAT INDEX

High temperatures combined with high **humidity** make hot weather seem even hotter. The U.S. government uses its **Heat Index** to calculate how air temperature will feel. Air temperature and humidity are measured, and then whether the measurement is in or out of direct sunlight is taken into consideration. The U.S. government warns the public when it expects the Heat Index to reach 105.8 degrees Fahrenheit or more for at least two days in a row.

◄ Qingdao, China, during a spell of hot weather in 2006. When the weather is hot, people often crowd onto beaches to enjoy the warmth and sunshine.

Where is hot weather most common?

Places along the **Equator** have the warmest climates. These areas are called the **tropics** and they have tropical climates. Daytime temperatures in the tropics can reach around 95 degrees Fahrenheit throughout the year. However, these temperatures are normal, so they are not a heat wave.

RECORD HEAT WAVE

In the summer of 1923 to 1924, the temperature in Marble Bar, Australia, reached more than 100 degrees Fahrenheit for 160 days in a row. Marble Bar often gets high temperatures, but this was a world record.

▼ The different climates of the world. The warmest areas are those nearest the Equator.

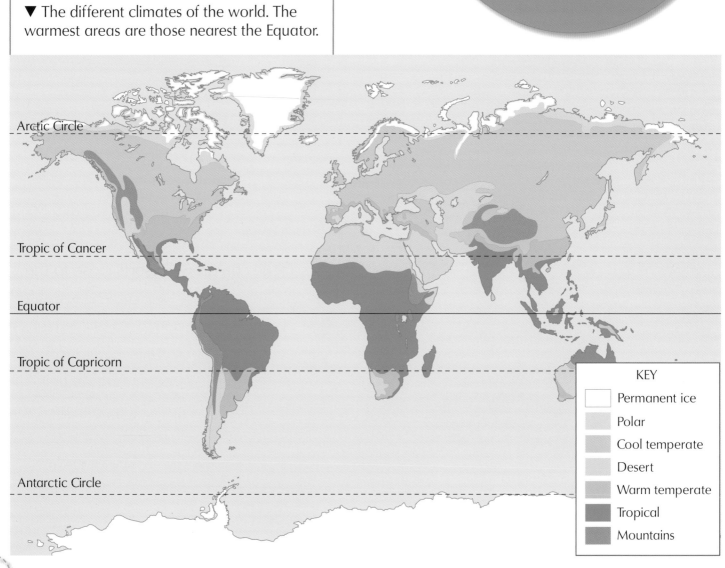

Arctic Circle

Tropic of Cancer

Equator

Tropic of Capricorn

Antarctic Circle

KEY
- Permanent ice
- Polar
- Cool temperate
- Desert
- Warm temperate
- Tropical
- Mountains

TROPICAL CLIMATES

Some tropical climates are the most humid climates in the world. They have heavy rainfall, especially at certain times of the year, and they feel sticky and uncomfortable most of the time. Even at night, temperatures may never drop much below 71 degrees Fahrenheit because thick clouds hold the heat from the Sun close to the Earth's surface. This happens in the great tropical rain forests, such as those around the Amazon River in Brazil, the Congo River in West Africa, and in Indonesia. Other tropical climates are drier, at least for part of the year. In these areas, there are often vast areas of grassland, such as in the African savanna.

▲ In a tropical rainforest, the warm temperatures and heavy rainfall provide perfect conditions for thick vegetation to grow.

▼ Few plants or animals can survive in the hot, dry environment of Death Valley, California.

HOT DESERTS

A **desert** is where the climate is very dry, so little can grow. Deserts close to the Equator, such as the Sahara Desert in Africa, can have some of the highest daytime temperatures in the world— more than 122 degrees Fahrenheit. The highest recorded temperature was 136 degrees Fahrenheit in El Azizia, Libya, on September 13, 1922. Desert temperatures may drop sharply at night because there are few clouds to trap the warm air near the Earth's surface.

Why do some places get warm weather?

The main factors that affect how warm a place normally gets are the **latitude**, the **altitude**, how far from the ocean it is, and the time of year.

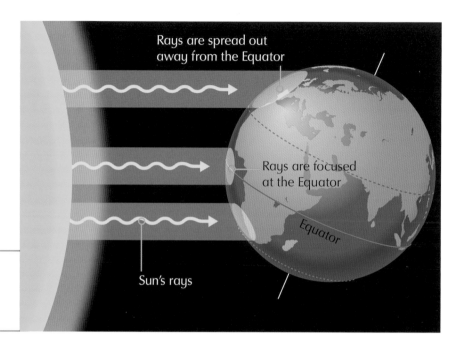

Rays are spread out away from the Equator

Rays are focused at the Equator

Equator

Sun's rays

▶ Close to the Equator, the Sun is very strong, which makes the weather warmer.

▼ Although Mount Kilimanjaro, Tanzania, lies close to the Equator, its summit, or top, is covered in snow.

LATITUDE

Latitude is how far north or south of the Equator a place is. Near the Equator, it is hotter because the Sun's rays reach the Earth most directly there. Further from the Equator, the rays strike the Earth at an angle, so they are more spread out and not as strong.

Altitude measures how high above sea level the land is. At high altitudes, the air is cooler than lower down. The temperature at the foot of a mountain can be very warm, but it may never be warm at the top.

WIND AND WATER

Land warms up faster than water. The warm air above the land rises. Near the coast, cooler air from the sea moves in to take its place, keeping coastal areas cool. Inland, away from the cool sea winds, air temperatures tend to be higher.

SEASONS

The **seasons** winter and summer occur because the Earth is tilted slightly on its **axis** as it travels on its yearly journey around the Sun. For part of the year, the northern half is closer to the Sun, and it is summer there. As the Earth continues on its journey, the southern half tilts toward the Sun, so it is summer in the south and winter in the north.

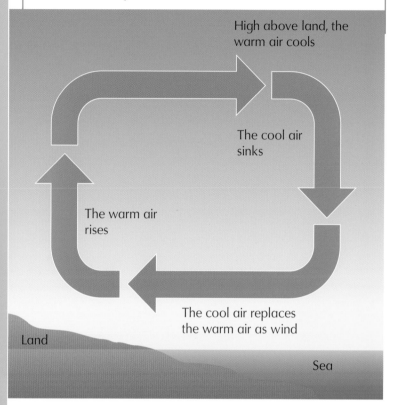

▼ Wind occurs when warm air rises and cooler air moves across the Earth's surface to take its place.

High above land, the warm air cools

The cool air sinks

The warm air rises

The cool air replaces the warm air as wind

Land

Sea

▼ The Earth is tilted on its axis. Temperatures are warmer when the Earth tilts toward the Sun. At this time, it is summer.

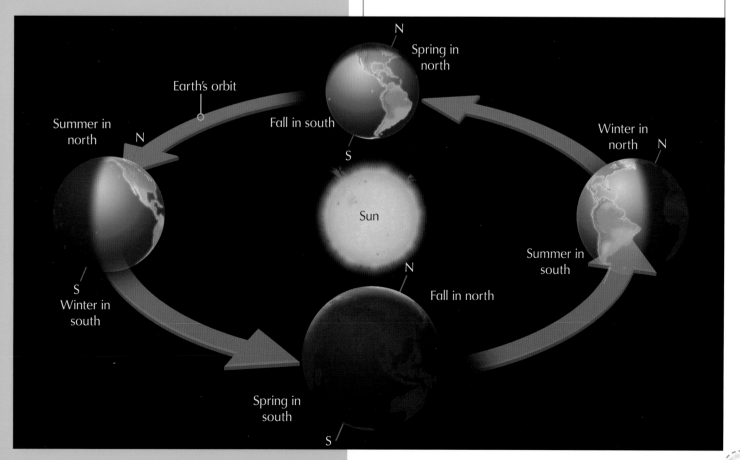

Earth's orbit

N
Spring in north

Summer in north

N

Fall in south

S

Sun

Winter in north
N

S
Winter in south

N

Fall in north

Summer in south

Spring in south

S

What causes a heat wave?

The Earth is surrounded by a blanket of air called the **atmosphere**. The atmosphere is in layers, and the weather happens in the bottom layer. During a heat wave, warm air becomes "stuck" over a region of the Earth's surface, leading to long periods with high temperatures.

◄ The Earth is surrounded by a blanket of air called the atmosphere. This is where weather takes place.

STATIONARY AIR

Normally, as the Sun warms the Earth, the air above it warms and rises. Cooler winds rush in, bringing rain, which helps to cool the Earth's surface and the air above it. If the warm air remains stationary, it blocks cool air and rain—and a heat wave occurs.

► During a heat wave, warm air remains over a region for days on end, with no cooler air, clouds, or rain to bring the temperature down.

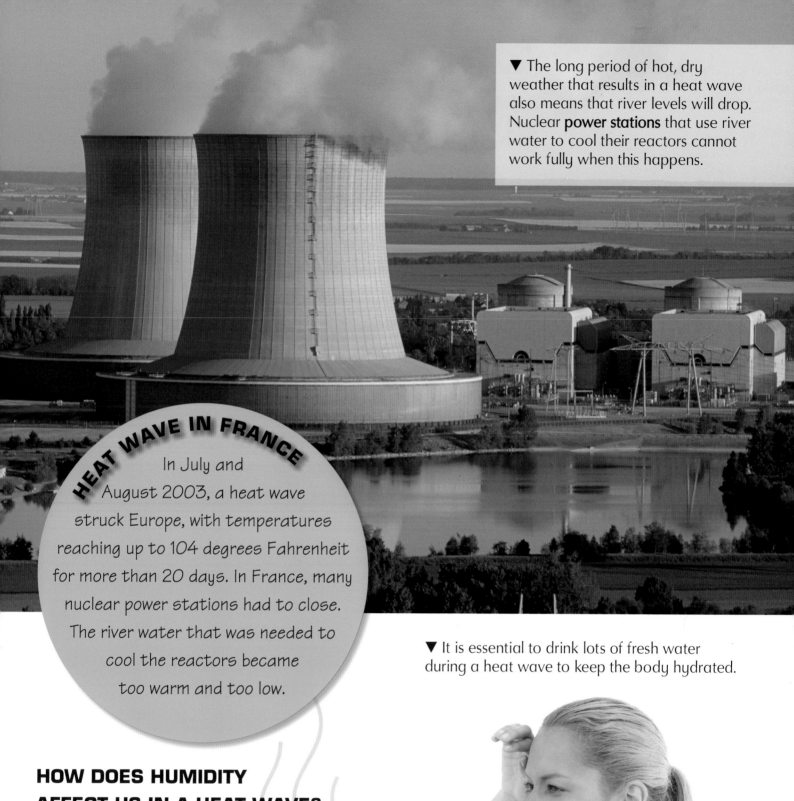

The long period of hot, dry weather that results in a heat wave also means that river levels will drop. Nuclear **power stations** that use river water to cool their reactors cannot work fully when this happens.

HEAT WAVE IN FRANCE

In July and August 2003, a heat wave struck Europe, with temperatures reaching up to 104 degrees Fahrenheit for more than 20 days. In France, many nuclear power stations had to close. The river water that was needed to cool the reactors became too warm and too low.

It is essential to drink lots of fresh water during a heat wave to keep the body hydrated.

HOW DOES HUMIDITY AFFECT US IN A HEAT WAVE?

When humans **sweat**, water in the body passes out through the skin and **evaporates** to cool the body down. However, when it is humid, there is already a lot of moisture in the air, so the air cannot absorb much more. Therefore, when humans sweat, it remains on the skin, making us feel sticky and uncomfortable. Our skin cannot cool down, so we feel much hotter.

11

Modern life

Many ways have been found to cope with the problems that unusual weather can bring, but very hot weather can still make modern life difficult.

▼ **Photochemical smog** hovers over El Paso, Texas. This white mist is caused by sunlight reacting with car exhaust fumes.

SMOG

When warm air is trapped over a city, strong sunlight reacts with gases from car exhausts and forms a thick, white mist called photochemical smog. This can hurt people's eyes and cause breathing problems. Today, new cars are usually made so that their exhausts give off fewer harmful gases.

RAIL AND ROAD

Driving in hot weather can be dangerous because roads can become damaged. **Tarmac** melts and car tires can burst on extremely hot surfaces. Metal expands when it is hot, which causes great problems on the railroads. In the past, rails were short, with small spaces between them, so that they could expand safely. Today, they are longer, without the spaces. The metal is treated and laid in ways that help to stop the rails expanding too much. However, if the metal does expand, it has no space to move into, and may be forced out of shape. If this happens, trains cannot use the rails, as there is a risk of accidents.

▲ Sticky, melted tarmac from roads and sidewalks is impossible to remove from anything it clings to.

URBAN HEAT ISLANDS

Cities tend to be much hotter than the countryside around them. These are called "urban **heat islands**." They form because the bricks and concrete of a city absorb heat from the Sun during the day, and then release it at night. This keeps temperatures high and allows a steady build-up of heat. Lack of wind and the heat given out by air conditioning systems and other machinery add to this effect. In Chicago in July 1995, temperatures reached 105 degrees Fahrenheit by day and only dropped to 84 degrees Fahrenheit at night. This led to more than 500 deaths in five days.

▼ This aerial picture shows the heat given off by buildings in an urban area in red. The cooler vegetation areas are shown in green.

Wildfires

In hot, dry weather, trees and grasslands become very dry. Wildfires, or forest fires, can easily start and spread very quickly.

▼ A wildfire threatens beachside homes in Malibu, California, in 1993.

HOW A WILDFIRE SPREADS

Wildfires are sometimes started on purpose, but they are mainly the result of mistakes— for example when someone drops a cigarette. If grass, or the sticks and leaves on the forest floor, are dry, they can soon catch fire. In hot weather, such fires will burn even more easily. Once it has started, a wildfire spreads rapidly as embers and sparks are carried on the wind. It can be extremely difficult for firefighters to stop the flames spreading. Nearby trees and grass soon catch fire so, as soon as one fire is under control, another may break out close by.

▶ A firebreak in New Zealand has been made by cutting down a strip of trees in the middle of the forest.

PREVENTING FIRES

In some countries, when the weather is hot and dry, special warnings remind people not to take risks. Camp fires, barbecues, and smoking in the countryside may be forbidden. Sometimes, strips of forest are cut down to make spaces that the fires cannot cross. These are called **firebreaks**.

HELP AT HAND

Fighting wildfires can be too much for local emergency services. They often need help from other parts of their country—or even from abroad. In 2007, the Greek fire services were helped by Russian "water-bomber" aircraft. Each plane can release 42 tons of water over a fire—as much as 525 bathtubs!

▼ A low-flying aircraft drops fire retardant onto the wildfire to try to put out and control the flames.

GREEK TRAGEDY

In the summer of 2007, temperatures in southern Europe reached more than 104 degrees Fahrenheit for many days, with little rain. In southern Greece, there were nearly 200 forest fires on the dry hillsides. More than 60 people died and firefighters came from across Europe to help put out the flames.

Human health

Heat waves are one of the most dangerous kinds of extreme weather. U.S. government figures show that more people die from the effects of heat than from any other natural disaster.

HEAT STRESS

In hot weather, it important to keep cool by staying in the shade, wearing light-colored clothes, and drinking plenty of clean water. This helps to avoid health problems called **heat stress**. This can include cramps, **heat exhaustion** and, most seriously, **heat stroke**.

HEAT STROKE

Heat stroke occurs when the body's temperature rises dangerously. If body temperature rises above 104 degrees Fahrenheit and it cannot be cooled, a person may go into a coma and die. Also, high temperatures and not being able to sleep during hot nights can put a strain on the heart.

◀ For older people with weak hearts and poor blood circulation, high temperatures bring an increased risk of heat stroke.

OTHER HEALTH PROBLEMS

People who sunbathe may burn their skin if they do not use **sunscreen**. In the long term, this can result in skin cancer. Diseases, such as **malaria**, are also spread by insects that breed in hot climates. Stomach problems can also be caused by hot weather because germs breed in food that is going bad. In poor countries, a heat wave results in a shortage of clean drinking water. People may be forced to drink water full of germs that cause killer diseases, such as **cholera**.

▲ Sunscreen filters out the harmful rays from the Sun, and helps to prevent sunburn and long-term damage to the skin.

SAFETY IN HOT WEATHER

Drink plenty of fluids to make up for the moisture your body loses as you sweat. Close blinds and curtains to shade rooms, and open windows to let fresh air in.

▲ Certain kinds of mosquito that live in hot climates can carry malaria. This is a dangerous disease that kills up to two million people a year.

Food and farming

Animals and plants also suffer during a heat wave. Often they cannot find water or food, and without shade, there is no escape from the heat.

▲ Animals in zoos are often given their food in blocks of ice. This helps them to stay cool.

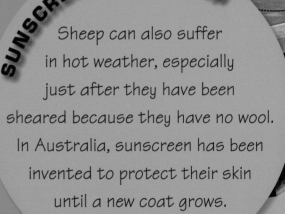

SUNSCREEN FOR SHEEP

Sheep can also suffer in hot weather, especially just after they have been sheared because they have no wool. In Australia, sunscreen has been invented to protect their skin until a new coat grows.

KEEPING ANIMALS COOL

Animals can die from heat stroke, too. During a heat wave in California in 2006, temperatures rose to more than 114 degrees Fahrenheit. Farmers had to find ways of keeping their animals cool, including giving them showers. However, more than 25,000 cattle and 700,000 chickens died. In the end, the estimated cost of the heat wave to farmers was more than one billion dollars.

▼ A farmer in South Carolina examines his **crops**, which have been killed by a period of very hot, dry weather.

WILTING PLANTS

Plants can be affected in hot weather. Lettuce leaves may burn, or the whole plant may "bolt" —the stems grow long and the lettuce leaves turn bitter, so they cannot be eaten. Tomatoes and other fruits and vegetables may be scorched. If temperatures are very high, some fruits, such as plums, stop growing, and so the crop is small.

ALGAE

Some living things do very well in hot weather, and this may also be harmful. For example, huge quantities of tiny plants called algae may form in stagnant water. They produce a thick, green scum on the surface. Some kinds of algae are poisonous.

◀ In hot weather, the amount of **duckweed**, a small plant, can double in size daily. In 2006, it covered more than 5 miles of a canal in London, England.

Drought

A **drought** is a long period of time without rain. The ground becomes dry and crops, animals, and people can die from lack of water.

WATER SHORTAGE

During a drought, more water is used, especially when temperatures are high. Crops and plants are in danger of dying unless they are watered. Governments advise people to save water in case shortages occur. For example, people are sometimes forbidden from using hosepipes because they waste water quickly. Every drop of water is needed for washing and drinking and to keep farm animals and crops alive.

▲ In dry parts of the world, wind-driven pumps bring water up from underground **boreholes**.

◄ In parts of Africa, a drought can mean that everyone must help to bring water from distant streams and wells.

▼ During a drought, rivers may appear to dry out completely. However, it may be possible to find water under the surface of the **riverbed**.

YEARS OF DROUGHT

In countries where droughts are common, people may harvest, or save, water during the rainy times. In one region in Zimbabwe, Africa, villagers have cut underground tanks out of the rocks to store rainwater. However, when a drought goes on for a long time, there is a limit to what people can do to overcome the problems. By April 2007, after several very dry years, Australia began to suffer greatly. Farmers needed help from the government to keep their farms going. Water in one of the country's main rivers, the Murray-Darling, was too low to flow out to sea properly. In some places, kangaroos came into people's gardens to look for food and water.

Heat and wildlife

Some plants and animals are adapted to live in hot, dry climates. They have developed ways to survive when other living things would find the conditions very difficult.

ANIMALS

Many desert animals are nocturnal, remaining hidden underground during the heat of the day. In the summer, some animals lose part of their coat—this is called molting. Some frogs and turtles **aestivate**, or sleep. They wake up when cooler, wetter weather arrives.

▼ Fish crowd into the shallows in a **reservoir** near Los Angeles. High temperatures can lead to a loss of **oxygen** from water. Fish become distressed and may die in large numbers.

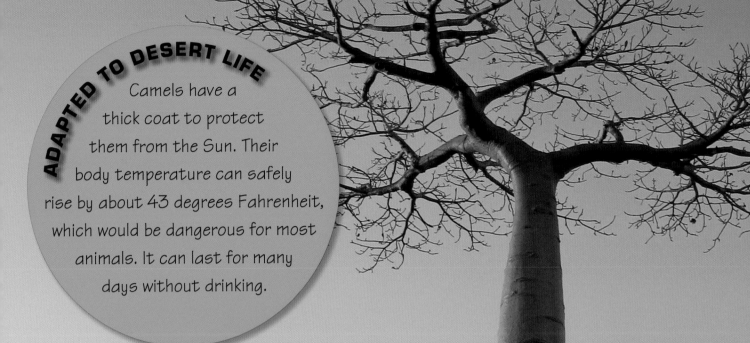

PLANTS

Many tropical plants have thick, waxy leaves so that they do not lose much moisture through evaporation. Others, such as **cacti**, store water in their swollen stems. The baobab tree grows in Africa and other hot, dry parts of the world. A mature baobab can store more than 31,700 gallons of water in its trunk—that is 700 bathtubs of water! The tree also saves water by losing all of its leaves during the dry part of the year, so that it looks almost dead. When the rains come, it grows leaves, flowers, and then fruit.

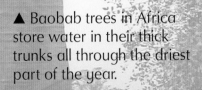

▲ Baobab trees in Africa store water in their thick trunks all through the driest part of the year.

Living with hot weather

People who live in hot countries have found ways to protect themselves from high temperatures by adapting their clothing and homes.

CLOTHING

In warm parts of the world, people wear garments that allow air to move around the body. It is best if these are made of absorbent material, such as cotton, which soaks up sweat. Light colors also **reflect** the Sun's rays, whereas dark colors absorb the heat. Where the Sun's rays are very strong, many people keep their skin covered, so that it does not burn.

▼ People who live in the desert protect themselves from the strong rays of the Sun by wearing loose, light-colored clothing.

AIR CONDITIONING

Many modern homes use air conditioning. This is a way of artificially cooling the air before it reaches the inside of a house, in a similar way to a refrigerator. Air conditioning uses a lot of electricity, so in a heat wave, power cuts may occur.

HOMES

Traditional homes are often designed to keep people comfortable. Thick mud or stone walls prevent heat from the outside world entering the home. Small windows on both sides of a building keep out as much sunshine as possible, while allowing air to flow through the building.

▼ In Coober Pedy, Australia, many homes are built underground. They remain cool during summer, when average temperatures are above 86 degrees Fahrenheit.

▼ The white walls of homes in countries such as Greece reflect the heat, keeping the houses cool inside. **Shutters** on the windows provide shade and allow air to pass through them.

Knock-on effects

Periods of unusually warm weather can cause long-term damage to the way plants and animals live together and depend on each other. When this happens, the **ecosystem** in which the animal or plant lives is harmed.

CORAL REEFS

Colorful coral reefs are home to large numbers of fish and other wildlife. People depend on this wildlife for food, and also for the money they get from tourists who visit the reefs.

▼ Coral is normally covered with colorful algae. However, when the seawater around it becomes too warm, the algae die, leaving the coral white in color.

COMPLICATED ECOSYSTEMS

Coral reefs are made up tiny living things, covered by colorful algae. The algae are also living creatures and they provide food for the coral. If the water is too warm, the algae leave and the coral turns white. When the water cools, the algae may return. However, if the temperature remains just two degrees Fahrenheit above normal for more than a couple of months, the coral starts to die and the damage is permanent.

▼ If birds nest too early in the year due to warmer weather, the young birds will suffer if temperatures return to normal.

SEASONS OUT OF CONTROL

In cooler parts of the world, warmer weather in winter can damage ecosystems. Warm weather may encourage birds to nest and rear young early, before there are enough insects to feed on. If the weather turns cold again, the young may die.

FRUIT FARMS

Warm winter weather can create all sorts of problems for fruit farmers. If temperatures are high, some trees may come into bloom early. Then cold temperatures may suddenly return. Blossom may die, without ever being able to form fruit later in the year.

▼ A spring heat wave can bring early blossom, which can be damaged if cold temperatures return.

Are heat waves getting worse?

The Earth's climate is getting warmer. This is called **global warming**. It has been happening at a greater speed in recent years. Scientists believe that the rising amount of **greenhouses gases** is the cause.

HEAT WAVE IN THE ARCTIC

In the summer of 2007, parts of the Arctic had a heat wave. Temperatures are normally no more than 40 degrees Fahrenheit, but they rose to more than 68 degrees Fahrenheit.

Sun's rays are reflected

Heat escapes

Sun's rays

Sun's rays are trapped, which warms the atmosphere

▲ The Sun warms the Earth and certain gases, such as carbon dioxide, trap some of the heat in the atmosphere. They act like the glass in a greenhouse.

GREENHOUSE GASES

The Sun heats the Earth's surface, which then warms the air above it. Greenhouse gases in the air trap this heat—similar to the way a greenhouse traps heat. Humans are burning large amounts of **fossil fuels**—coal, gas, and oil. This produces **carbon dioxide**, one of the main greenhouse gases. At the same time, many trees, which absorb carbon dioxide, are being destroyed. Some scientists think that temperatures could rise as much as 44 degrees Fahrenheit in the next 100 years because we are burning too much fuel.

THE FUTURE

Rising temperatures may make weather very unpredictable, with more storms, flooding, and heat waves. Warmer temperatures in the **Arctic** and **Antarctic** have already resulted in much of the ice there melting. This could make sea levels rise, flooding low-lying countries. With higher temperatures, there could be more disease, and it may be harder to grow enough food. Global warming is already happening, but we must try to stop it getting worse.

▼ Global warming could mean that **locusts**, which devastate crops in the tropics, could spread further afield.

▲ As temperatures in the Arctic and Antarctic rise, large masses of sea ice begin to **calve**, or break up, and melt at a greater speed than normal.

Glossary

AESTIVATE
To fall into a kind of deep sleep during hot, dry weather.

ALTITUDE
The height above sea level.

ANTARCTIC
The region around the South Pole.

ARCTIC
The region around the North Pole.

ATMOSPHERE
The blanket of air around the Earth.

AXIS
An imaginary line through the middle of the Earth from the North Pole to the South Pole.

BOREHOLE
A hole drilled deep into the ground to find water or minerals.

CACTUS
A desert plant with a thick, fleshy stem.

CALVE
When a glacier or sheet of sea ice breaks up, it is calving.

CARBON DIOXIDE
One of the gases in the air. Carbon dioxide is produced when fuel is burned.

CHOLERA
A disease of the stomach and intestines, with severe diarrhea. Untreated, it can kill very quickly.

CROP
Plants grown by farmers to be used in some way, for example, as food.

DESERT
A region with little rain and few plants.

DROUGHT
A long period without rain, or with very little rain.

DUCKWEED
A kind of small plant that grows in still, fresh water.

ECOSYSTEM
The way in which animals and plants in a particular area are related to each other and to their environment.

EQUATOR
An imaginary line around the middle of the Earth, halfway between the North Pole and the South Pole.

EVAPORATE
To change from a liquid into a gas.

FIREBREAK
An area of cleared land created to prevent fire from spreading, for example through a forest.

FOSSIL FUELS
Coal, oil, and natural gas. These fuels were formed millions of years ago from the remains of plants and marine animals.

GLOBAL WARMING
Increase in the average temperature of the air around the Earth. Global warming is caused by an increase in greenhouse gases, such as carbon dioxide, in the air.

GREENHOUSE GAS
Gas in the air that traps the Sun's heat. Greenhouse gases include water vapor, carbon dioxide, and methane.

HEAT EXHAUSTION
Dizziness, weakness, and other mild health problems that happen when the body is too hot.

HEAT INDEX
A way of measuring how hot the air actually feels.

HEAT ISLAND
A place where temperatures are higher than in surrounding areas.

HEAT STRESS
A range of problems caused by the body becoming too hot. It includes heat exhaustion and heat stroke.

HEAT STROKE
Collapse caused by too much heat—the most dangerous form of heat stress.

HUMIDITY
The moisture in the air.

LATITUDE
The distance a place is north or south of the Equator. It is measured in degrees.

LOCUST
A kind of grasshopper. Locusts sometimes gather in huge swarms and destroy crops.

MALARIA
A disease caused by parasites that is spread by a type of mosquito. It causes high fever, and can kill.

OXYGEN
A gas in the air that living things need in order to survive.

PHOTOCHEMICAL SMOG
A mist caused by the action of sunshine on chemicals from car exhausts.

POWER STATION
A building in which electricity is generated.

REFLECT
To cast back light.

RESERVOIR
An artificial lake used for storing water.

RIVERBED
A channel in the ground through which a river flows.

SEASON
A period of the year, such as spring, summer, fall, and winter. In some parts of the world, there are also wet and dry seasons.

SHUTTERS
Movable covers for windows.

SUNSCREEN
A skin lotion containing chemicals that can block the harmful rays from the Sun.

SWEAT
Moisture that passes out through the skin when we are warm.

TARMAC
A road surface made with tar.

TROPICS
Part of the world on each side of the Equator between the Tropic of Cancer and the Tropic of Capricorn.

Index